Carnival Time!

Written by Janine Scott
Photography by Joe Viesti

The Caribbean

Each year in February, people in Puerto Rico and many other parts of the Caribbean celebrate carnival time. It is a time of fun and friendship. Alberto and his best friend Hector get together at Alberto's to make carnival masks. Then the boys join the street parade and have fun with their family and friends!

friendship   making and keeping friends

Contents

Carnival Time!

Alberto lives in Ponce in the south of Puerto Rico. It is the home of one of the largest carnivals in Puerto Rico. Every year, his mother and father help with the carnival. They have a workshop in their house where family and friends gather to make their papier-mâché masks for the street parade.

papier-mâché   a mixture of paper and glue that hardens as it dries

Does your city
or town hold
a famous event?

Alberto's best friend, Hector, makes his mask there, too.
It takes a great deal of time and patience. The masks
have long horns, teeth, and tongues. The boys use
a special mold to form the face. The West Africans
who first came to Puerto Rico made similar masks.
The boys think that making the masks is as much fun
as the carnival itself!

It also takes a great deal of time and work to make carnival costumes. Besides scary masks and costumes, some people wear outfits that are decorated with feathers, beads, and sequins. The outfits are often very beautiful—and very big! Some headdresses are almost as tall as the people wearing them. A carnival princess wearing one of these costumes must be helped up onto the stage if she is crowned Carnival Queen.

Each February, Ponce residents open stalls to sell homemade masks and other carnival items. People from all over Puerto Rico travel to Ponce to join in the celebration. Some people buy masks to wear for the street parade, and others buy them as souvenirs. Alberto and Hector like looking at the masks, but they both think that the masks they are making are the best!

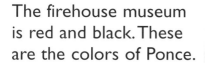

The firehouse museum is red and black. These are the colors of Ponce.

With many out-of-towners, Alberto's family takes time to visit the famous firehouse museum in Ponce. Carnival costumes and masks are on display there every year. The boys gather many good ideas for their own masks from the museum visit.

Many cultures have masks. What are your favorite kinds of masks?

9

Finally, it's carnival time! The boys hurry to the main plaza for the daytime carnival celebrations. They see people everywhere dressed in scary masks and loose "clown" suits with lots of ruffles. Everyone's mask is different. Many costumes and masks are yellow and red, which are the colors of the Spanish flag. Spain once ruled Puerto Rico, so Spanish is still the main language. Some people wear red, white, and blue costumes and masks. These are the colors of the Puerto Rican flag.

Did You Know?

The masks in the Ponce carnival are a blend of African, Spanish, and Caribbean cultures. The blend creates a special Puerto Rican tradition. The masks are called vejigante (*vay hee GON tay*) masks.

African masks

The carnival is not only about scary masks. Many special events take place, such as the competition of the carnival princesses for the title of Carnival Queen.

This year, Alberto was lucky to be chosen to present the crowns to the carnival princesses and queen.

One of the highlights of the carnival is when the carnival princesses parade through the streets at night.

Explore the Caribbean

The Caribbean is also known as the West Indies. It is a chain of islands divided into three main island groups. One of these groups, the Bahamas, has about 3,000 small islands and reefs. Many of the islands in the Caribbean were formed long ago by volcanoes.

The Caribbean is near the equator. It has warm weather all year round. Trade winds blow all year round, too. These can bring heavy rains and hurricanes.

Palm trees grow in the Caribbean. Their strong, flexible trunks bend and sway in the wind.

Christopher Columbus first arrived in the Caribbean in 1492. He thought he had landed in the East Indies islands of Asia. Many years later, the islands were renamed the West Indies when the mistake was discovered.

equator   an imaginary line that is halfway between the North and South Poles

Cuba is the largest island in the Caribbean. The capital of Cuba is Havana. The city has many high-rise apartment buildings.

On the Go!

Which styles of music first came from the Caribbean?
Go to page 18

Which sport did the English introduce to the Caribbean?
Go to page 20

Why did the Notting Hill Carnival start in London?
Go to page 22

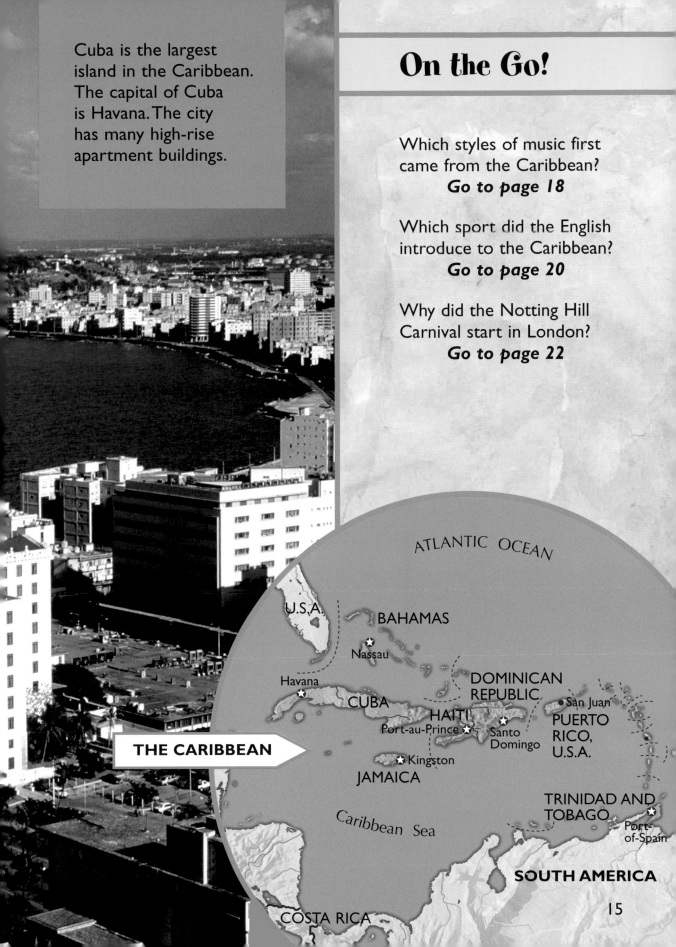

ATLANTIC OCEAN

U.S.A.

BAHAMAS

Nassau

Havana

CUBA

DOMINICAN
REPUBLIC

San Juan

HAITI
Port-au-Prince
Santo
Domingo

PUERTO
RICO,
U.S.A.

THE CARIBBEAN

Kingston

JAMAICA

TRINIDAD AND
TOBAGO
Port-
of-Spain

Caribbean Sea

SOUTH AMERICA

COSTA RICA

Plenty of Plantations

The warm, tropical climate of the Caribbean is perfect for growing crops. The soil is rich, and the land receives plenty of rainfall. There are many large plantations in the Caribbean. Many crops are grown on these plantations and then exported to other parts of the world. Sugar cane, an important crop, was first introduced to the Caribbean during the 1500s. Today, Cuba is a leading producer of sugar cane.

Other export crops include bananas, coffee, and spices. Spices are a popular ingredient in Caribbean creole cooking. This kind of cooking is a blend of African and European styles, such as French and Spanish.

Sugar cane plantation

plantation   a large farm where crops such as sugar, coffee, tea, bananas, and cotton are grown

16

Bananas grow well in the warm climate of the Caribbean. There are many kinds of bananas, and not all of them are yellow or green. The Red Jamaica is a small red banana!

17

Island Music

The Caribbean is the home of calypso music. This lively music started in Trinidad in the 1800s. Today, it combines American jazz with African and Spanish music styles. Steel-pan drums are an important part of calypso and were first made from old oil drums. Another style of music popular in the Caribbean is reggae, which first came from Jamaica.

Limbo dancing is also popular in the Caribbean. Dancers have to bend over backward and dance under a bar. The bar is gradually lowered to make dancing under it more difficult. Sometimes the bar is even set on fire!

Oil drums are not only made into steel-pan drums in the Caribbean. They are also made into barbecues for grilling meat over charcoal.

Fun and Games

In the Caribbean, people spend a great deal of time outside because the weather is so mild. Many people enjoy playing a variety of sports, some of which were introduced by Europeans many years ago. The game of cricket was brought to the Caribbean by the English. If a grass field is not available to play on, people can use the beach.

Jamaica surprised the world in 1994 when a sports team from this very hot country did well in a very cold sport—bobsledding. The team earned 14th place in the Winter Olympics. It was a great achievement for a country without ice or snow!

Salt Lake City Winter Olympics, 2002

The West Indies cricket team plays internationally. The team is made up of players from many of the Caribbean countries.

Carnival on the Move

Caribbean customs are alive in other parts of the world, too. Many people from the West Indies settled in London in the 1950s. Their first carnival, which was organized in 1959, was held in a hall. By 1964, however, the carnival had grown and moved to the streets of Notting Hill in London. It is now one of the biggest street parades in Europe.

custom   a special way of doing things

A Caribbean calypso carnival is not complete without whistles and horns. Children and adults blow them to create a special carnival sound.

Get Ready, GO!

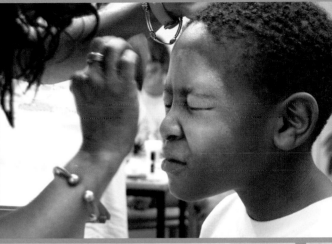

Up to a million people from many different cultures come to London to enjoy the carnival's Caribbean flavor. There are colorful costumes, lively music, and Caribbean food. An important part of the celebration is Children's Day. It is a fun-filled day for both children and adults.

What Do You Think?

1   Why do you think people celebrate carnivals and festivals around the world?

2   Why were the friendships Alberto had leading up to carnival time and during the carnival parade just as important as the carnival itself?

What makes friends and friendship so special?

Index